First Science

Keeping your Balance

The authors would like to thank Sevenoaks Discount Cycles for lending the bike on page 14.

Editorial planning: Serpentine Editorial
Scientific consultant: Dr. J.J.M. Rowe

Designed by The R & B Partnership
Illustrator: David Anstey
Photographer: Peter Millard

Additional photographs:
Chris Fairclough Colour Library 18, 31; ZEFA 11 (bottom),
15 (top and bottom);
Peter Millard Library 11 (top);
David Exton/Trustees of the Science Museum 30.

First Science

Keeping your Balance

Julian Rowe
and Molly Perham

CHILDRENS PRESS®

CHICAGO

Contents

WHAT IS BALANCE? page 6

MAKING IT BALANCE page 8

BALANCING A LOAD page 10

SEESAWS page 12

HELPING TO BALANCE page 14

LOSING BALANCE page 16

BALANCE IN ACTION page 18

TUG-OF-WAR page 20

WEIGHING THINGS
page 22

SCALES page 24

BALANCING TRICKS
page 26

MAKE A MOBILE page 28

THINK ABOUT...
BALANCE page 30

INDEX page 32

 SAFETY WARNING

Activities marked with this symbol require the presence and
help of an adult. Plastic should always be used instead of glass.

What is balance?

How good are you at standing on one leg? See if you can count to ten before you start to fall over.

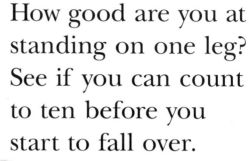

The skateboarder holds out his arms to keep himself steady. This helps him to balance.

This girl is balancing an apple on her head. What is she doing with her arms?

Making it balance

Can you balance
a tennis racket on
your hand? It is
not easy!

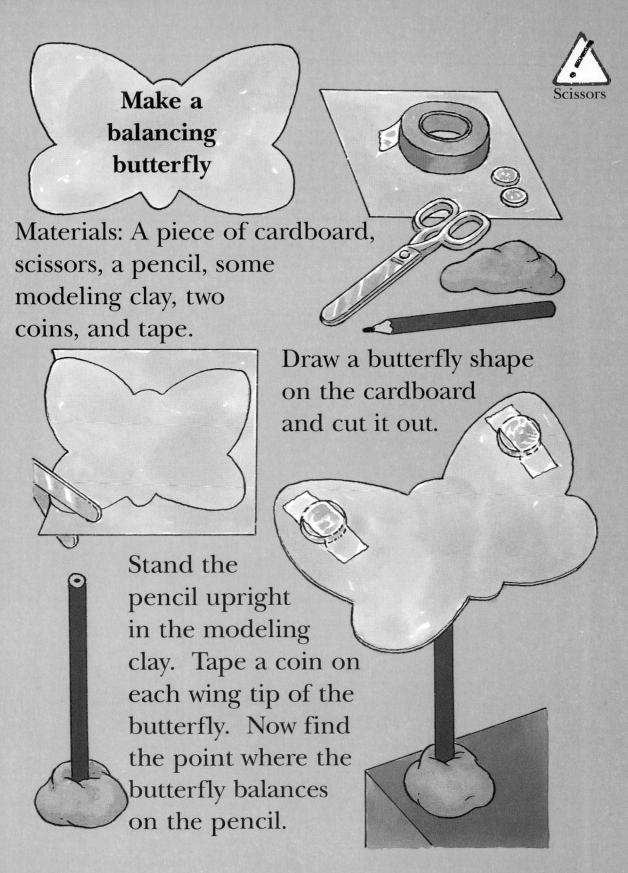

Make a balancing butterfly

Materials: A piece of cardboard, scissors, a pencil, some modeling clay, two coins, and tape.

Draw a butterfly shape on the cardboard and cut it out.

Stand the pencil upright in the modeling clay. Tape a coin on each wing tip of the butterfly. Now find the point where the butterfly balances on the pencil.

Balancing a load

Your balance point is in the middle of your body. Try carrying a heavy load in one hand. Can you keep your balance? It is easier to balance if you carry the load on your back.

The crane must balance. It has a very
heavy block on the short arm. This block
balances the weight of the long arm and
the load the crane
is lifting.

Animals are
sometimes used to
carry heavy loads.
The weight needs
to be evenly
balanced between
the two sides.

See-saws

If you sit on one end of a seesaw and two friends sit on the other end, does it balance?

What has happened now to make the seesaw balance?

Make a seesaw

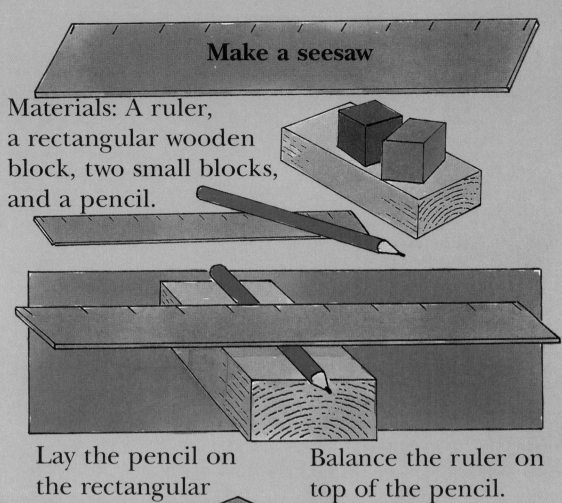

Materials: A ruler, a rectangular wooden block, two small blocks, and a pencil.

Lay the pencil on the rectangular block.

Balance the ruler on top of the pencil.

Put a small block at one end.

What happens if you also put a block at the other end?

What happens if you move one block closer to the middle?

Helping to balance

Can you ride a two-wheeler bike?
The small wheels at the back help you to
balance while you are learning. They are
called training
wheels.

Tightrope walkers
use long poles to
keep themselves
steady.

Its long heavy tail
helps the kangaroo
balance as it
springs along.

Losing balance

This girl is not very steady. What can she do to keep her balance?

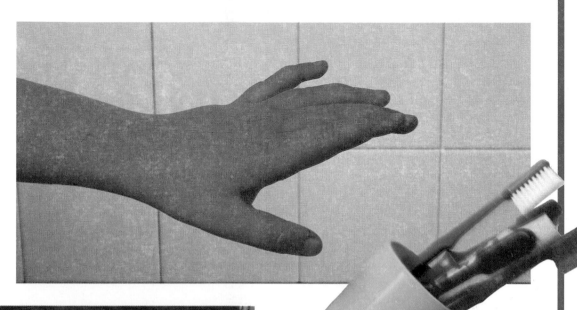

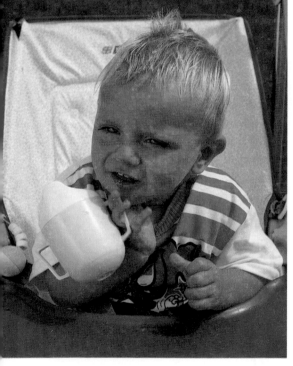

A small push makes this cup of toothbrushes lose its balance and tip over. It is too heavy at the top.

The baby's cup has a weight in the bottom to keep it steady.

Balance in action

A strong wind can blow a boat over. These people are leaning out to one side. Their weight balances the force of the wind.

A force called gravity pulls everything to the ground. A weightlifter has to push upward very hard to balance this force.

Tug-of-war

But if they all pull with the same force, the rope will not move. The forces will then be evenly balanced.

If the children on this side of the rope
pull harder than those on the other side,
the rope will move.

Weighing things

When you weigh something, you are measuring the force with which gravity pulls it down.

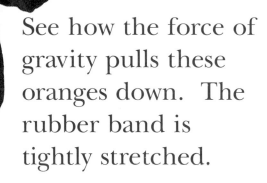

See how the force of gravity pulls these oranges down. The rubber band is tightly stretched.

Make a spring balance

Materials: A large rubber band, a small container, some marbles and corks, a ruler, and some wool or string.

Tie the container to the rubber band.

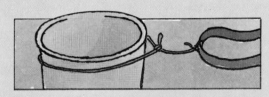

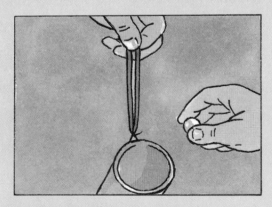

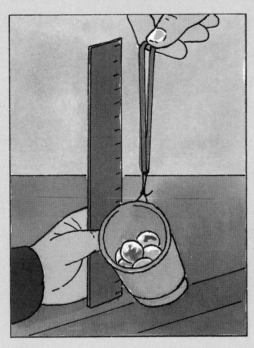

Fill the container with marbles.

Measure how far the band stretches.

Now fill the container with corks and see how far the band stretches.

Scales

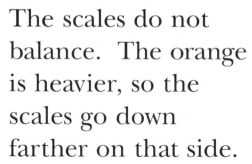

This girl is trying to guess whether the orange or the apple is heavier.

It is much easier to weigh them on some scales.

The scales do not balance. The orange is heavier, so the scales go down farther on that side.

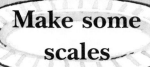

Make some scales

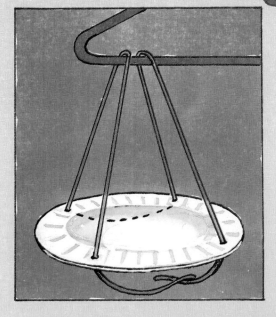

Materials: A coat hanger, two paper plates, and some string.

Hang the coat hanger from a hook. Make four small holes near the edge of each plate.

Thread string through the holes, over the coat hanger, and back through the holes. Tie the string underneath each plate.

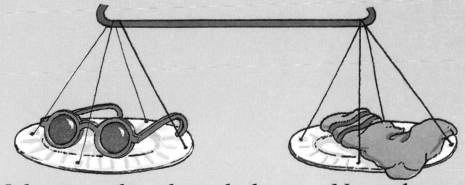

Make sure the plates balance. Now place different objects on each plate and see if you can make them balance.

25

Balancing tricks

Sit on a chair with your arms folded and your feet flat on the floor. Make sure your back is touching the back of the chair. Now try to get up without leaning forward.

Don't move your arms!

Stand close to a wall so that an entire side of your body touches it. Now lift your outside foot and balance on the other leg. Did you fall over?

Your balance point, or center of gravity, is in the middle of your body above your feet. In these two balancing tricks you can't keep your center of gravity above your feet, so you lose your balance.

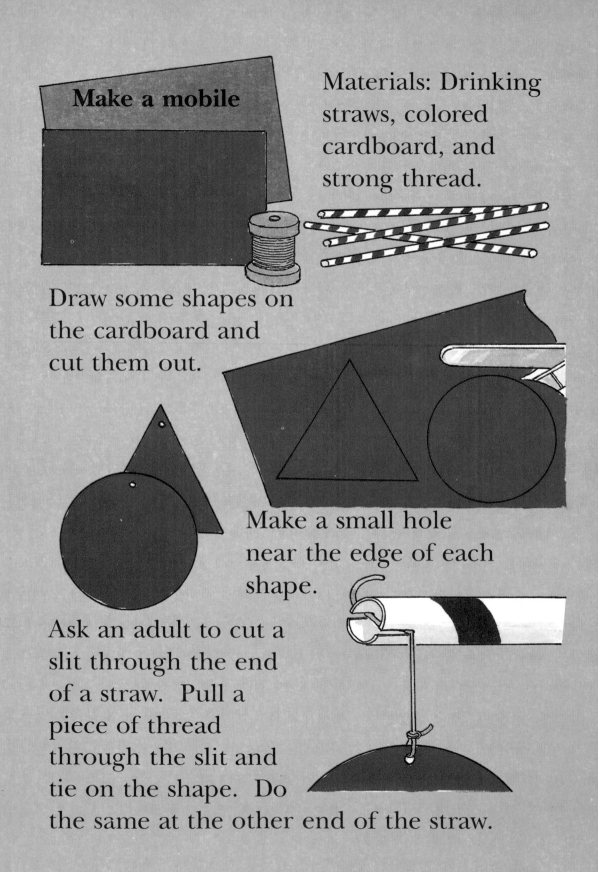

Make a mobile

Materials: Drinking straws, colored cardboard, and strong thread.

Draw some shapes on the cardboard and cut them out.

Make a small hole near the edge of each shape.

Ask an adult to cut a slit through the end of a straw. Pull a piece of thread through the slit and tie on the shape. Do the same at the other end of the straw.

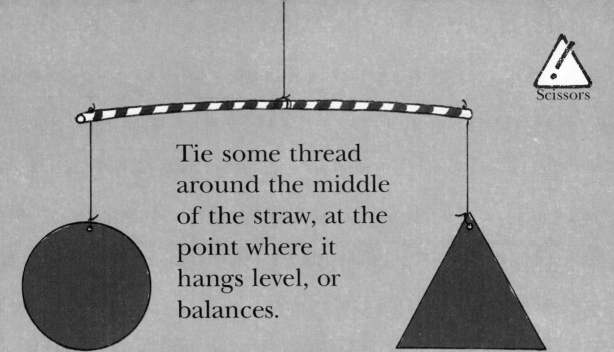

Tie some thread around the middle of the straw, at the point where it hangs level, or balances.

Attach this thread to the end of another straw. Keep adding shapes to your mobile until it looks like this.

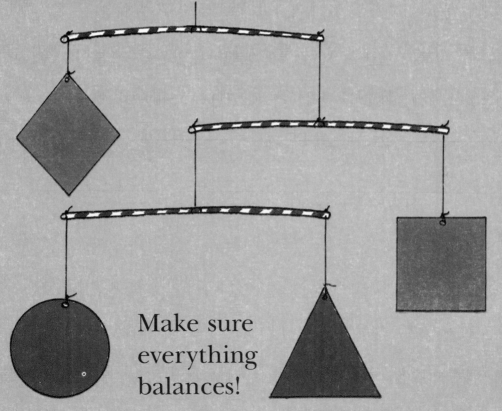

Make sure everything balances!

Think about...
balance

A heavy weight is pulled along the arm until the bar balances. The pointer shows how much the girl weighs.

Which bottle is the most stable? Which is the easiest to knock over?

This parrot has a long, heavy tail to help it balance on the perch.

Have you ever built a house of cards? You need to balance each card very carefully, or the house will fall down!

INDEX

animals, 11
apple, 7, 24
arms, 7, 11, 26
baby's cup, 17
back, 10, 26
balance point, 10, 27
bike, 14
boat, 18
body, 10, 27
bottle, 30
butterfly, 9
center of gravity, 27
chair, 26
crane, 11
falling over, 6, 27
feet, 26, 27
force, 18, 19, 21, 22
gravity, 19, 22, 27
ground, 19
hand, 8, 10
head, 7
heavy load, 10, 11
house of cards, 31
kangaroo, 15
leaning, 18, 26

leg, 6, 27
lifting, 11
mobile, 28, 29
orange, 24
parrot, 31
pole, 15
pulling, 19, 20, 21, 22
pushing, 17, 19
rope, 20, 21
scales, 24, 25
seesaw, 12, 13
skateboarder, 7
spring balance, 23
stable, 30
steady, 7, 15, 16, 17
tail, 15
tennis racket, 8
tightrope walkers, 15
training wheels, 14
wall, 27
weighing, 22, 24
weight, 11, 17, 18, 30
weightlifter, 19
wheels, 14
wind, 18